The BROWNIE Annual

Published by special arrangement with
THE GIRL GUIDES ASSOCIATION

Edited by ROBERT MOSS

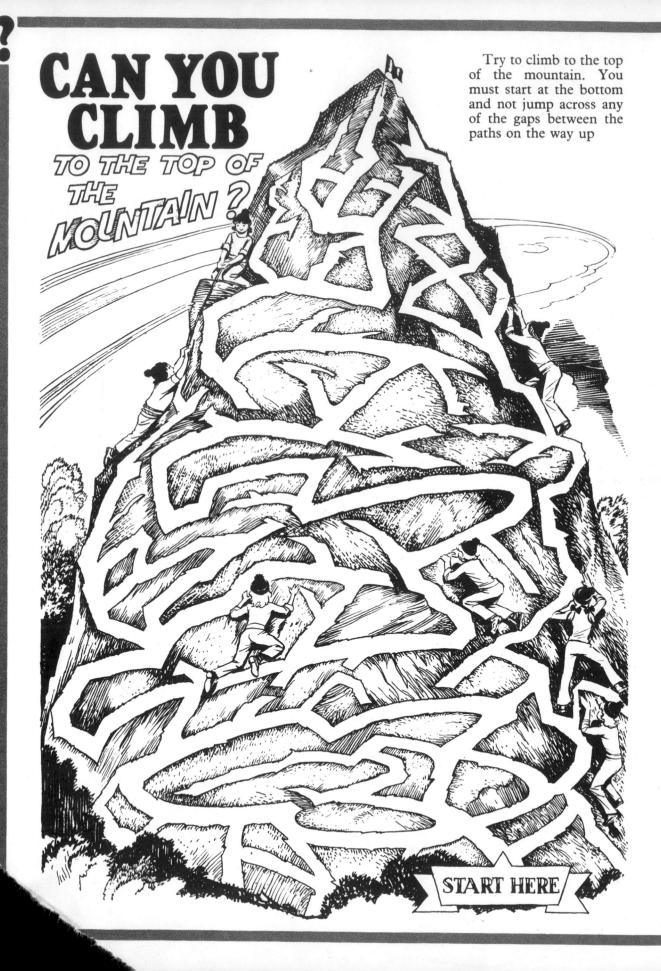

MAKE A DANCING BROWNIE MAN

For the Toymaker Badge

Phyllis Mead Tells You How in Words and Photographs

GIRL GUIDES

Clause 1 of the Toymaker badge invites you to "make a toy of your own choice". This Dancing Brownie man is fun to make and to play with.

You will need thick cardboard (cereal boxes are

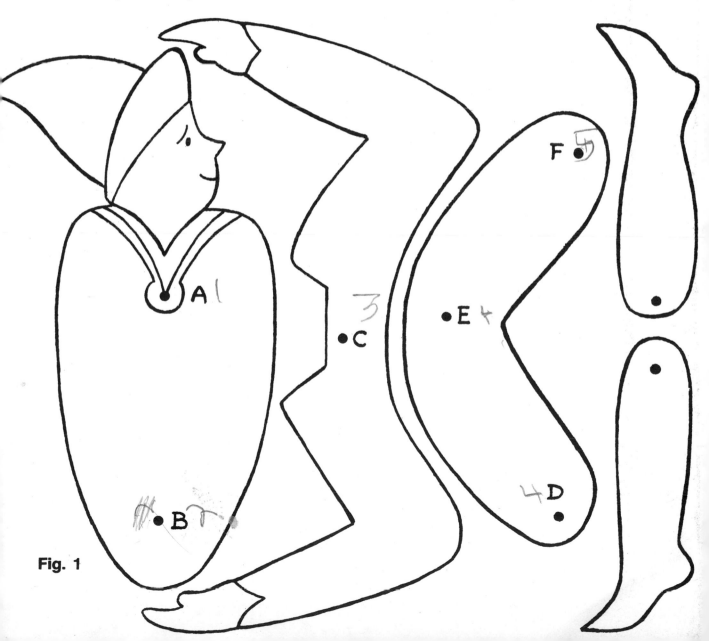

Fig. 1

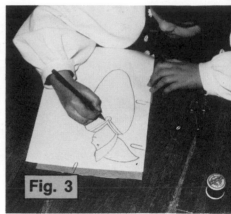

Fig. 2

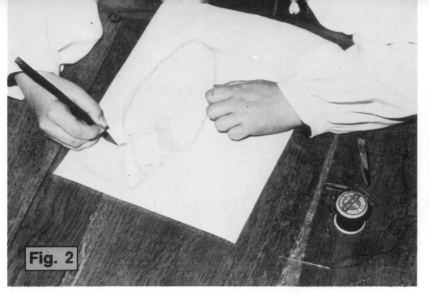

Fig. 3

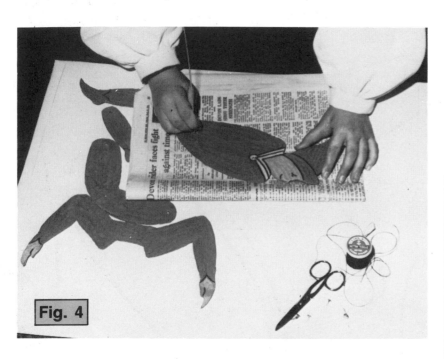

Fig. 4

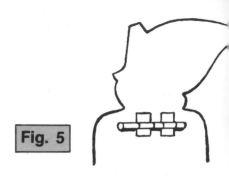

Fig. 5

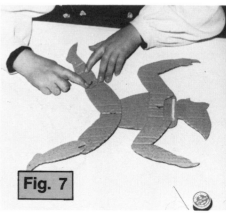

Fig. 7

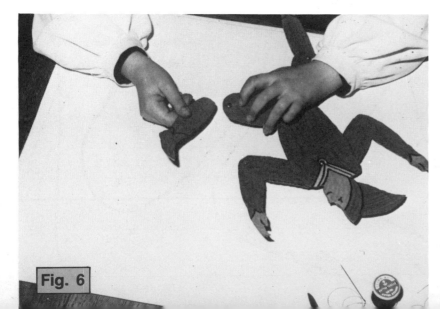

Fig. 6

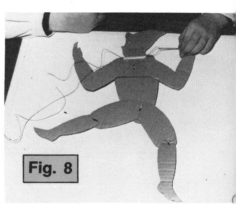

Fig. 8

too thin, but a strong shoe-box would do); paints or crayons; a darning needle; a black felt-tipped pen; a fine steel knitting-needle or a thin nail; a pair of scissors; a drinking straw; sticky tape; four push-through paper-fasteners; three or four slip-on paper-fasteners; black button-thread; a sharp pencil; tracing paper (Mother's greaseproof paper will do).

Carefully trace the outlines of the five parts *(fig. 1)* that make up the Brownie Man on to your tracing paper. Turn over the paper and scribble heavily over the back of the outlines you have drawn *(fig. 2)*.

Place the tracing, right side uppermost, on the cardboard. Pressing firmly, draw over the outlines of the figure *(fig. 3)*.

Cut out the five pieces.

Draw in the face, hat, boots, scarf and sleeves with the felt pen. Colour face, hands and costume.

Place the pieces on a thick wad of newspaper and pierce holes at A, B, C, D and E with the knitting-needle *(fig. 4)*.

Cut a piece of drinking straw 4cm long. Secure it to the back of the Brownie Man with sticky tape *(fig. 5)*.

Now join the parts of your Brownie Man together by passing the push-through paper-fasteners through the holes at A and C, B and E, D and G, and F and H *(fig. 6)*. Open out the fasteners at the back, but make sure that the arms and legs move very freely *(fig. 7)*.

Thread the darning needle with a long length of black thread. Push the needle through the drinking straw so that the Brow-nie Man will hang from the thread *(fig. 8)*.

Tie one end of the thread to a table-leg so that the Brownie Man's feet just touch the ground when you hold the cotton tight. Hold the thread between your thumb and second finger. By jerking the thread with your forefinger you will be able to make the Brownie Man dance.

With a little practice you will be able to make him dance backwards and forwards along the thread.

CAN YOU NAME THE BIRDS,

Suzanne's Guide sister is working for the Naturalist badge. With Suzanne's help, she has built a "hide" in the wood near their house so that she can watch birds, butterflies, and various other wild creatures. Suzanne is just as interested and watches with her. They both learn a lot of interesting things.

How much do *you* know about the birds, butterflies and moths pictured on these two pages? From the pictures of them and the descriptions at the foot of the pages can you name some of them?

1. Big bird, cock having tufts by its ears, shining green head, red cheeks, white-ringed neck and speckled red-brown body with long, barred tail; hen with shorter tail and dull brown speckled plumage. Nest hidden in ground. This bird is mostly seen in woods, where it is specially reared.

2. Smart, dainty bird with long black-and-white tail, white forehead, cheeks and underparts, black head and throat; tail wags up and down as it runs.

3. Insect-eating bird with swooping flight; shiny blue-black breast and back, light chestnut head, light-grey underparts, and long forked tail; builds nest of straw and mud, lined with grass and feathers, and set in rafters of barns; summer visitor only.

4. Small bird with blue crown, white cheeks, blue-green back and yellowish underparts; dark stripe across eyes; wonderful acrobat; with us all year round.

5. Big black bird with blue sheen on its feathers; nests high in trees with others of its kind; nest built of woven sticks and mud and lined with grass and straw; with us all year round.

6. Large blue-grey bird with long tail tipped with white; white breast barred with brown; lays eggs in other birds' nests; summer visitor only, heralding arrival in early spring by peculiar call.

7. Reddish-brown bird not often seen; summer visitor only; builds nest of grass and dead leaves and hides it in ground or in clump

MOTHS AND BUTTERFLIES?

by RIKKI TAYLOR

of brambles; sings at night as well as in day.

8. Moth with orange and brown colouring and a spot like an eye on each wing; often seen in daylight flying over moorland. The caterpillar is bright-green with dark markings.

9. Large moth with wing-span of 2½″ – 3″; grey-green wings with fawn markings and band of deeper colour across fore-wings. Caterpillar is green with yellow stripes along sides tipped with red; blue curved horn.

10. Beautiful moth with short, fat body; fore-wings brightly marked with brown and white; hind wings red with blue-black markings. Caterpillar is dark-brown and very hairy, hairs pricking skin if

handled without care.

11. Butterfly with orange-yellow wings with wide black borders; black spot on each upper wing; orange spot on lower. Female is paler. Likes clover fields.

12. Pretty butterfly with wings of orange-red against a pattern of yellow-and-black splashed with blue near tips; mostly seen in south of Great Britain.

13. Butterfly with black-and-scarlet wings splashed with white; seen everywhere in summer; likes orchards and the blossom of ivy, hop and thistle.

A BADGE FOR BELINDA

By Mary Reed

"Six, seven, eight, nine . . ." counted Susan.

Belinda's foot caught in the skipping-rope. She sighed, threw down the rope and flopped on the lawn.

"It's no good, Susan, I'll never do it. I can't skip sixty times forward, let alone sixty times backward!"

"It just takes practice," Susan replied, but secretly she agreed with Belinda.

Poor Belinda didn't skip at all well. She had been practising for weeks, hoping to win the Brownie Agility badge, but there had been no improvement at all.

Susan had several badges sewn on her Brownie uniform, but Belinda hadn't any. Belinda tried hard every time Susan worked for a badge, but whereas Susan sailed through her test, Belinda got nowhere.

Susan spent hours helping Belinda practise, so she couldn't help groaning when Belinda, having recovered her breath, jumped up and said, "Now let me practise leap-frog."

Obligingly Susan touched her toes.

Belinda took a long walk backwards and then began to run towards Susan. Susan tensed, expecting to feel Belinda's weight on her back, but Belinda screeched to a halt a few inches away from her.

"You're too high," she complained.

Susan crouched lower.

"Lower, lower!" shouted Belinda, until Susan felt that she was low enough for a flea to hop over.

Once again Belinda took a long run, but this time she crashed into Susan and sent her sprawling on the ground.

Belinda was full of apologies as Susan got up, dusting herself.

"It's no good, Susan; I'll never do it"

"I'm sorry! It's not fair on you. I ought to give up trying for the Agility badge, but I gave up last time, when we were working for the Dancer badge."

In spite of her grazed knee, Susan couldn't help smiling when she remembered how Belinda had wrecked all the folk-dances they'd tried. Belinda had no idea of keeping in time with the music and could never remember what she had to do. She always seemed to dance in the opposite direction from everyone else. Just then Belinda's mother hurried into the garden.

"Mrs Edwards has had to go out, and she's taken her toddler with her. They may be out for a long time, so I'm going to fetch her other children and bring them back for tea. Oh, dear, I wonder if we have enough food in the house for all of them?"

Belinda ran to her. "Don't worry, Mum. If you light the oven for us, we'll make something for tea."

Soon Belinda and Susan were putting on aprons in the kitchen. "I can bake shortbread best. What can you make?" asked Belinda.

Susan looked worried. "I've never baked before. I've never wanted to."

Belinda took a packet of cake-mix from the cupboard. "You'd better make small cakes, then. They're easy. You just add an egg and two tablespoons of water to the mix."

The girls were soon busy. Susan had never heard Belinda talk so much. Never having baked before, she herself needed to be told which utensils to use, how to beat the mixture, and how much mixture to put in the paper cases.

An hour later Susan, who'd been invited to stay to tea, was sitting round the table with Belinda and Mrs Edwards' three older children. The shortbread and cakes looked so tempting that no one needed a second invitation to help themselves.

At the end of the meal, Mrs Edwards arrived back with her toddler, Tim. Belinda and Susan cleared the table. Susan watched Belinda stack the plates and wash up. She looked quite grown-up, she was so efficient. As she took a cloth to dry the plates, Susan laughed. "Belinda, you've been so silly!"

Belinda looked amazed, as she couldn't think of anything she had done wrong.

"No wonder you have no Brownie badges!" explained Susan. "You've been trying to get the same ones as me. You've been trying all the things that I'm good at instead of doing what you can do best. You'd easily earn the Hostess, House Orderly and Cook badges."

Belinda gazed at her in surprise. Then: "I believe you're right. I hadn't thought of it like that. Come to think of it, we're all different and we don't have the same hobbies. Gosh, I'm going to talk to Brown Owl next week about working for those other badges—the Hostess badge first, I think."

Out in the garden again, she picked up her skipping-rope.

"Oh, no!" groaned Susan. "I thought you were going to work for your Hostess badge?"

"So I am," replied Belinda happily, "but I'll still practise skipping. After all, you never know, I might get better!"

Susan thought how a few hours before she had never thought of baking and yet had made some delicious cakes for tea. "Yes," she agreed. "You never know! Three, four, five . . ."

"Belinda," laughed Susan, "you've been so silly!"

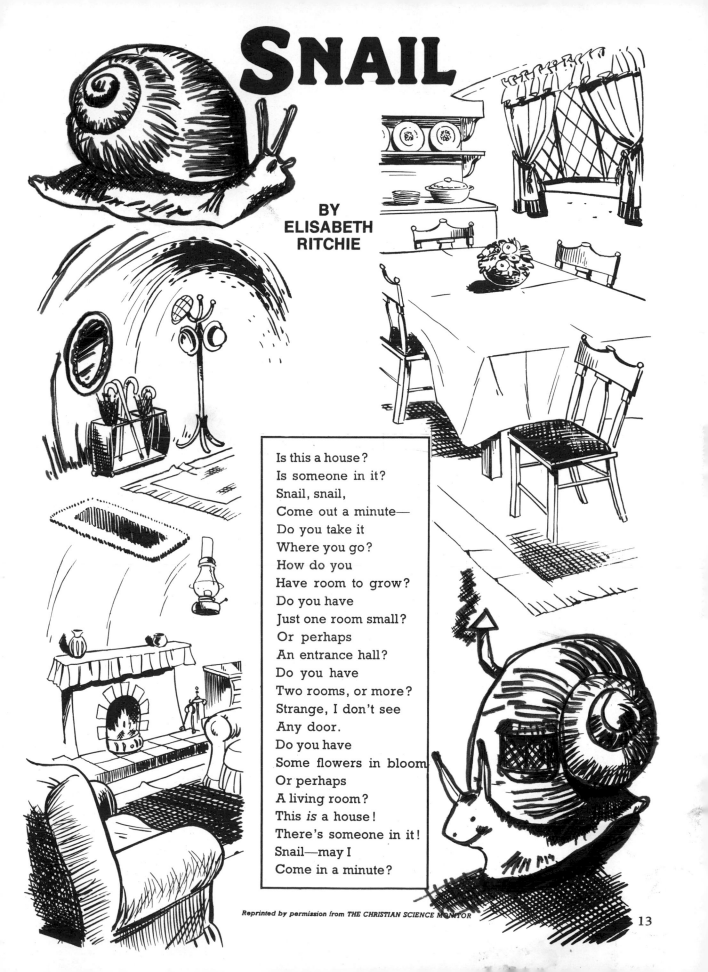

SNAIL

BY
ELISABETH
RITCHIE

Is this a house?
Is someone in it?
Snail, snail,
Come out a minute—
Do you take it
Where you go?
How do you
Have room to grow?
Do you have
Just one room small?
Or perhaps
An entrance hall?
Do you have
Two rooms, or more?
Strange, I don't see
Any door.
Do you have
Some flowers in bloom
Or perhaps
A living room?
This *is* a house!
There's someone in it!
Snail—may I
Come in a minute?

Reprinted by permission from THE CHRISTIAN SCIENCE MONITOR

ANIMALS OF THE COUNTRYSIDE

THE MOLE

Moles are underground creatures. You seldom see one, but you often see the molehills they throw up. They are small black creatures who live mainly on worms. Living underground, they are blind. Their velvety skin is sometimes made up into moleskin coats for ladies

THE HARE

Hares live above ground, whereas rabbits burrow below for their homes. The hare has long ears and can run fast. The saying "mad as a March hare" arises from the antics in spring of the hare, who leaps wildly about and uses his paws like a boxer

THE RABBIT

The wild rabbit is disliked by the farmer, whose crops it eats. Children often keep tame rabbits as pets. Rabbits live in burrows below ground and usually have large families

THE SQUIRREL

The grey squirrel is the kind usually seen in the British countryside, but some red squirrels still survive. The squirrel lives mainly on nuts, which he stores up for the winter. He doesn't go to sleep through the winter, as some people think

THE DEER

There are several kinds of deer in Great Britain. They can be seen in the New Forest, on Exmoor, in Scotland, in private parks, and elsewhere. They are shy creatures and keep away from people

THE FOX

The fox is well known for its cunning and is the enemy of the farmer, whose poultry it will raid if it gets half a chance. Fox cubs are charming to watch when at play. The main food of the fox is the rabbit, and since rabbits have become scarce many foxes have made their homes in the suburbs of towns. Foxes are still hunted in Great Britain, but many people think fox-hunting is a cruel sport

THE OTTER

The home of the otter is a "holt" in the bank of a river or stream. The otter is a wonderful swimmer and lives mostly on fish. Some fishermen say that otters ruin the fishing for them, but otter-hunts are not allowed to go on now. The otter is becoming rare in Britain and needs to be protected.

THE BADGER

You don't often see the badger; it is a creature of the night. Badgers are harmless animals and are the farmer's friend, for they eat pests that damage crops. They live below ground in "setts", which they keep spotlessly clean, changing their bedding of grass and leaves every day

THE WEASEL

Almost the only difference between the weasel and the stoat is in size, the stoat being larger. Both are fierce little creatures and kill and eat rats, mice and birds — and rabbits too

THE HEDGEHOG

The hedgehog comes out at night and roots about for food like the little hedge-pig he is. When danger threatens, he rolls himself into a prickly ball. He loves milk and will become quite tame if you leave a saucerful out for him each evening. He is a useful chap to have in the garden, which he will keep free of slugs and other pests

THE MOUSE

The dormouse, the harvest mouse and the fieldmouse are all mice who live out of doors. The dormouse sleeps through the winter. The harvest mouse makes its nest on the stalks of growing corn. The fieldmouse lives in a hole in a grassy bank or under the roots of a tree

THE SHREW

Shrews are tiny, mouselike creatures with large appetites. They feed on insects and soon die if they stop eating

THE VOLE

The vole is a rodent that lives in a meadow or in the bank of a stream or river. It does much damage because it eats the farmer's crops, young shoots and greenstuff. The water-vole is a fine swimmer and diver

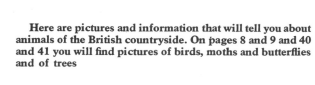

Here are pictures and information that will tell you about animals of the British countryside. On pages 8 and 9 and 40 and 41 you will find pictures of birds, moths and butterflies and of trees

My Brownie Friends

by the Editor

The Brownie holding the kite in the picture on the opposite page is Penny Shaw, and behind her are Joanna Hopkins, Clare Brooker, and Juliette Taylor. They'd just joined in the Teddy Bears' picnic. I hadn't been invited, so all I could do was creep in when they weren't looking and take their photograph.

All four Brownies belong to the 15th Cheltenham (St. Peter's, Leckhampton) Pack. They live near me, but I have Brownie friends in many different parts of the country. I made new friends when I spent an evening with the Sutton Courtenay Brownie Pack, Oxfordshire, and showed them colour slides I had taken of Brownie and Guide activities.

One Brownie Guider asked me to open their jumble sale, as she was sure that lots of people would come to it just to see what the Editor of the *Brownie Annual* and the *Girl Guide Annual* looked like! Well, I can tell you that the people who came were so eager to snap up the bargains that they didn't bother to look at me or listen to my opening speech, which I had to cut short to "I now declare the jumble sale open"!

Every summer I go to the headquarters of the Gloucester-shire Girl Guides at Cowley Deer Park, where I meet Brownies and Guides and take pictures of them pitching tents, climbing rope-ladders, crossing rope bridges, cooking, and, without fail, eating ice-cream. The Brownies always insist on showing me their Pack holiday house, and climb up on to their bunk-beds to show me how lovely it is to sleep there, especially in the top bunk, for which, to avoid squabbles, they take turns.

Brownies of Herefordshire gave me a nice welcome when I drove to Eastnor Castle, near Ledbury, for their Revels, and an even nicer and most unusual

The Editor with Brownie friends

Colour slides by Robert Moss

16

on the wall of my office, which is now covered with pictures of Brownies and Guides.

It will show you how wide-awake Brownies are when I tell you that I was walking up the stairs one day at CHQ, which is the London headquarters of the Girl Guides Association and means Commonwealth Headquarters, when one of the Brownies in a visiting Pack stopped, looked hard at me, then said in a whisper to a friend, "That man is in my *Brownie Annual*."

She was right, too, except that it was my picture and not me!

Well, even if I don't happen to meet you at CHQ or visit your Pack, we do know each other through the *Brownie Annual*, through which I send you my best wishes for a wonderful year of Brownie Guiding. —— *R.M.*

The Brownies share the Teddy Bears' picnic

Ready to fly the *Brownie Annual* longtailed kite

farewell when I left. One of the highlights of the Revels was a medieval dance, with all the Brownies in costume. Against the background of Eastnor Castle it was a most impressive and colourful display, and at the end two of the Brownies in rich and beautiful old-time costume came and bade me farewell by dropping me a graceful, old-fashioned curtsey!

Although I have only visited a few of the nineteen thousand Brownie Guide Packs in the United Kingdom, I hear from quite a number of them, and thousands of Brownies send in entries for the thrilling prize competition that appears each year in the *Brownie Annual*. Sometimes they send their photograph, and I put each one

Brownies Make Things

A Tin For String
by M. I. Eckhardt

This is a simple but useful article to make for the home. You will need a tin suitable for holding a ball of string; coloured paper; braid; Bostik or other adhesive; string, and scissors.

Ask a grown-up to make a hole in the lid for you. Then cover the lid with coloured paper, finishing neatly round the hole (fig. I).

Cover the tin with coloured paper, glueing carefully so that the paper does not wrinkle. Decorate with different shapes of coloured sticky paper, or use a packet of shapes.

Cut two pieces of braid to fit

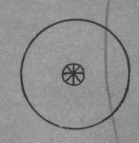

exactly around the tin at the top and at the bottom. Put Bostik or other adhesive around the top and bottom of the tin first, and

then press your braid firmly on.

Place the ball of string in the tin, threading the end through the hole in the lid to complete.

An Easter Card
by Daphne M. Pilcher

All you need is some white card or fairly heavy paper and one brass push-through paper-fastener.

Make yourself templates of the two parts of the card and draw round them carefully. Cut

them out and decorate them suitably, drawing in the chick, etc., as shown in the diagram.

Put in the paper-fastener at **A** and you have an Easter-egg card which, when opened, shows the chick.

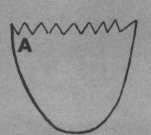

Dolls' Coathangers
by M. P. Wallington

All you need for these is a packet of pipe-cleaners.

Fold one of the pipe-cleaners so that it looks like diagram no. 1. Now twist each "arm" tightly to make the hanger stronger, as diagram 2.

You can make as many others as you have pipe-cleaners. They will be just right for hanging up your dolls' clothes.

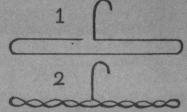

STRANGE TRAIN

by JEAN KENWARD

It did not run from here to there
    Or even there to here;
It only ran from where—to where?
    Or just from far to near.

It did not run from this to that,
    Nor yet from thence to thither,
But came from no one gathered what
    And then departed hither.

And who sat in that train at all
    Or what their destination
None knew, nor did the driver call
    The name of any station.

And as it went upon its way
    With noisy engines thrumming
"You think I've gone?" it seemed to say,
    "But others think I'm coming!"

MAKE AND DRESS THESE FIGURES

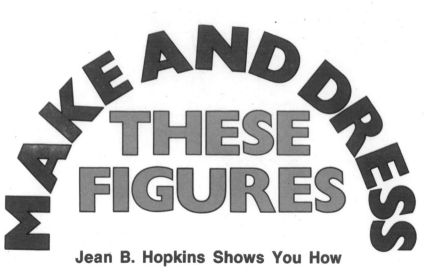

Jean B. Hopkins Shows You How

All you need are thin cardboard (perhaps a cereal box), a pencil or pen, scissors, bits of material, some wool, and glue or flour-paste.

First draw a simple figure shape on the cardboard, then cut it out.

Now cut out some clothes, and stick them on. You could make a clown like the one illustrated. Blue material would make a Guide. I've used brown to make a Brownie. You could make a family of father, mother and baby, or characters from a nursery-rhyme or a story and use them as puppets in a play—perhaps for the Jester badge.

The Christmas Story

By the 4th Christchurch Brownies and Guides

The Nativity

Mary and Joseph

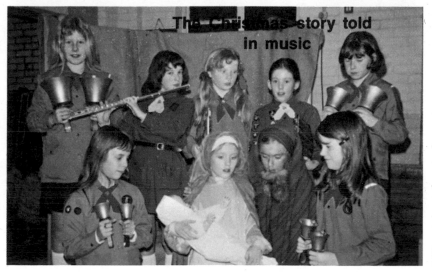
The Christmas story told in music

Colour prints by Miss G. Aslett

WHERE IS TUCKTONIA?

It's a Place Where All the "Sights" of Britain Can Be Seen at Once

If you haven't yet seen most of the famous showplaces of Great Britain —like Buckingham Palace, Stonehenge, and Stratford-upon-Avon—you can do so by paying a single visit to Tucktonia, in Christchurch, Dorset.

This astonishing place covers three and a half acres and presents all the chief "sights" of Britain on a tiny scale. It is a fascinating "Tom Thumb" landscape. All the models are made of fibre-glass or wood, and the whole cost over a million pounds to create.

You can see famous London buildings like the Houses of Parliament, St Paul's Cathedral, and the Tower of London. Outside London there are Stonehenge, Blackpool Tower, Brighton Pier, Scottish castles, and the white cliffs of Dover. It's all most realistic.

The pictures on these and the two following pages show some of the places reproduced at Tucktonia. —R.M.

Tower Bridge, London, opens to allow the passage of a tug and a train of barges

"I'm the King of the Castle!" cries this boy, but the castle is Windsor Castle, and it's the Queen who lives there

The Houses of Parliament and Big Ben, with children who are almost able to touch the famous clock

Nelson on his column in Trafalgar Square, London. The only figures missing are the pigeons!

Stonehenge, the famous prehistoric monument on Salisbury Plain—but now also in Tucktonia, Dorset

This is a model of part of London in the days of William Shakespeare, whose plays were first performed at the Globe Theatre, London

Buckingham Palace, with the Victoria monument in front of it

The Tower of London

St. Paul's Cathedral, Sir Christopher Wren's famous church in the City of London

25

FUN AT THE FAIR

Nora Windridge Offers Some Bright Ideas for Use at the Guide Bazaar or During Brownie Revels

Teddy Bear Competition

Invite Brownies and visiting children to enter their Teddy Bears in a simple competition. This would be very popular. There could be prizes for the most handsome bear or the biggest or the smallest or the best-dressed.

You will need numbered tickets. Pin a number on to each Teddy Bear as he is handed in and write down the number of the owner's name in a notebook: TEDDY BEAR NUMBER 5: OWNER, MARY JONES; TEDDY BEAR No. 8: OWNER, CHRISTINE HOLMES; TEDDY BEAR No. 11: OWNER, ROSA DEAN, and so on.

You could have different classes, such as DRESSED and UNDRESSED TEDDY BEARS, TEDDY BEARS UNDER 30.5 cm (12″), TEDDY BEARS OVER 30.5 cm.

Prepare cards to pin on the winning bears—first, second and third, if there are enough entries, and ask a grown-up who knows about Teddy Bears to be the judge.

Painting the Balloons

You will need good, round balloons, blown up, for this amusing competition, and string, scissors, felt pens or other markers, scraps of felt, fur or other material, strong adhesive, and a clothes-line and pegs.

Competitors have to paint the balloons. When painted, the balloons can be pegged to the clothes-line. This adds gaiety to the scene. Award prizes for the cleverest balloon face, or for the prettiest, or for the funniest, or for the ugliest, and so on.

Older brothers and sisters and grown-ups could be allowed to enter the competition if they are blindfolded! This should produce lots of fun.

The pictures on this page show some of the funny faces that might be done by competitors.

Silhouette Puzzle

Find Her Name

You can find the name of this Dutch girl if you arrange the letters on her dress correctly

—*Irene Urquhart*

RIDDLES

What goes through a door but never goes in or out?
The keyhole.

What question can never be answered by "Yes"?
"Are you asleep?"

What has ears but doesn't hear?
Wheat.

What are these Brownies doing? If you can guess from the silhouettes you will know what Interest badges they are working for

PACK HOLIDAYS ARE GREAT

It isn't all play on Pack holiday, but washing socks is fun when you do it together

Colour prints by Miss W. J. Beer

Portsmouth Brownies on Pack holiday look eagerly through scrapbooks sent by pen-friend Packs in New Zealand

The Christchurch Brownies gather flowers—and a few more pets

Colour print by Miss G. Aslett

Making paper dolls passes an enjoyable hour or two

Colour print by Miss W. J. Beer

This thirsty lamb enjoys the 4th Christchurch Brownies' Pack holiday, as he gets well fed

Wash-day isn't really a chore on Pack holiday

Colour prints by Miss G. Aslett

South Croydon Brownies (6th and 8th Packs) smile as they peel

Colour slide by Miss E. Banks

Olney Brownies leave a record of their holiday in the Worthing sands

Colour print by Mrs Brown

FROM US TO YOU

SPOTTED BROWNIES
At the Clay Cross Division Revels the theme is "Disneyland", and these Brownies of the 1st Shirebrook (Holy Trinity) Pack have become dalmatians, though not 101 of them

Photo: The Derbyshire Times

African Brownies at Revels in Rhodesia wave to all their sister Brownies overseas

Photo: Mrs J. Harwin

Baby Sister

Speedwells are blue as summer skies,
And that's the blue of Baby's eyes.

Daisies have the pinky tips,
And that's the pink of Baby's lips.

A field of golden corn shines fair,
And that's the gold of Baby's hair.

Soft are the petals of a rose,
And soft are Baby's hands and toes.

Sweeter than honey from the bee,
My little sister is to me.
—*Francis Cartwright*

My Wish

I wished a little wish one night
And now it has come true.
I was my Mummy's only child;
Now she possesses two.
I have a little sister new,
So pretty and so small.
I very gently kissed her cheek—
My wish, wrapped in a shawl!
—*Honor Hoggan*

PET PALS

Hebe Spaull tells some true stories of strange friendships

A basket made for two

Dogs don't like cats, birds are frightened of cats, and cats regard mice as something to be caught and eaten! That is the general belief about these "natural enemies". Yet there have been many friendships between creatures who are usually antagonistic to each other. Mother cats have been known to befriend baby rabbits and other creatures whom they might be expected to chase and eat.

A farmer's family had a pet turkey who became the inseparable friend of the family cat. Regularly every day they were to be seen patrolling the farmyard together. It must have been a quaint sight.

A cat named Figaro and a raven named Horace always slept in the same basket and were the best of friends.

Another unusual friendship was between a hen and two kittens. The kittens invariably settled down to sleep under the wing of Mother Hen.

An Oxfordshire family had a cat and a tame jackdaw as pets. To everybody's surprise, the two became the closest friends. They insisted on sleeping together and were seldom seen apart.

Another cat and bird friendship was between a cat and a parrot. They would sit side by side on the parrot's cage. Kitty called on Polly every morning, and then they put their heads together and chatted.

A collie dog was left in charge of a small poultry farm. His job, as he knew quite well, was to keep away foxes, rats and other enemies. But he seemed to feel a special responsibility for the chicks and encouraged young chicks to come and nestle in his fur in the sun when the wind was chilly.

An old farm-horse named Boxer used to take the farm kitten and puppy for regular rides on his back. The three were the best of friends.

A Cornish cat had all her kittens taken from her. She was very upset and made several unsuccessful attempts to steal another cat's family to take the place of her own. Then one day this cat located a moorhen's nest with six youngsters in it. One by one she brought the fluffy black chicks back home and placed them gently in a box in her owner's kitchen, watching over them with loving care!

Budgie keeps watch while pussy sleeps

Kitty feels safe and sheltered under those ears

"Oh, do come and play!" the lamb urges its friend the calf. "It's just the day for a romp"

Noddy, a pet owl, helps the old dog to guard the house and has even learned to bark!

"Keep still while I climb up." Trixie the fox doesn't mind being used as a stepping-stone by his friend the pussy

Photographs by Alan Band Associates

The puma cub wants to play leapfrog, but Snowy, the rabbit, isn't keen

"What shall we do today?" asks Atalanta, the golden eagle, to her friend, Shep, the sheep-dog. They live together on a farm in North Wales

MANDY'S WEATHER STATION

By Sybil Josty

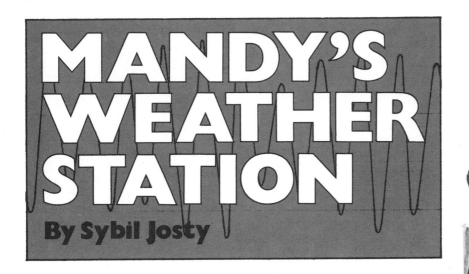

Ilma, who was a keen Guide, had returned from camp full of tales of singsongs, campfires, games and expeditions. She was especially keen on the weather-station her Patrol had made to record weather conditions while they were under canvas.

She told her young sister, Mandy, all about it. Mandy listened eagerly. She was a Brownie, and looked forward to joining Guides, which she would be old enough to do after her next birthday.

"I'm going to make a weather-station in the garden," said Ilma. "It'll be a birthday present for you from me, and you can help me build it."

Mandy agreed. She was delighted with the idea.

"Pity we can't use that garden next door," said Ilma. "We could put up a marvellous weather-station there, and have grand games among the bushes as well."

Mandy nodded. The house next door was old, and the garden was large and rambling, with a high wall all round it. She had often looked at it from her bedroom window, and thought what

fine games they could play there among the shrubberies and in the large wild garden beyond the flower-beds. What a waste, she thought, to have a garden like that and nobody to play in it! In the long summer holidays it was particularly tantalising, as their own garden was tiny, a patch of lawn with a row of apple-trees at the bottom.

"It's no use thinking about that," Ilma remarked. "Old Mr Bennett lives there on his own. I asked him once if he had any jumble for the Guides, but he was grumpy and said no. I haven't been there since."

"Let's make a list of the things

we shall want for our weather-station," suggested Mandy.

Ilma explained that they could start with a rain-gauge, a weather-vane, and a thermometer.

"What do we want for the rain-gauge?" asked Mandy.

"An empty milk-bottle and a funnel," replied Ilma. "You put the funnel into the bottle, and stick it out in the open where it'll catch all the rain. We'll have to mark it in centimetres along the side of the bottle so that we can see how much rain we've had."

"I know!" cried Mandy eagerly. "We'll make a graph, and mark down how much rain falls each week."

35

"Good idea!" said Ilma. "We'll do the same for the temperature. If we could get one of those maximum and minimum thermometers we had at camp we'd know how cold it had been in the night."

They felt excited about their new project, and could hardly wait to start the next day. Mandy knew where to get the bottle and funnel, and Ilma said she would buy a thermometer. The only thing they had to make was the weather-vane.

"Let's put it on the end of the garage roof," said Ilma. "That would be good because it faces south, so it will be easy to tell the direction of the wind."

The next day they made an early start. Ilma knew exactly what to do. With Mandy's help, she put a ladder against the end of the garage. Then they fixed two pieces of wood flat like a cross, marking the ends NORTH, SOUTH, EAST, and WEST. In the centre they hammered an upright rod. Then they fastened a piece of wood, pointed at one end, on top of the rod, so that it swung freely. They stepped back to admire their handiwork. They watched breathlessly until the arrow began to move.

"Look, Mandy," Ilma called jubilantly, "it's swinging to the south-west!"

They grinned at each other. They carried the ladder to the end of the garden. They had obtained permission to fix their thermometer to the trunk of one of the apple-trees. Ilma climbed the ladder, and fastened the thermometer high up with a strong piece of wire. She peered over the wall into next door's garden. She had a good view of the large garden-shed, where old Mr Bennett spent much of his time.

"Come down and let me have a look," called Mandy.

Ilma came down, and Mandy took her place up the ladder. "I wonder what he does in that shed," she said, when she came down.

"You sometimes hear him sawing wood—that's what it sounds like, anyway. I can see him from my bedroom window, going in and out, and he's always puffing at his old pipe."

"It's a marvellous garden," sighed Mandy. "I'd love to explore it."

They forgot the garden in the pleasure of beginning their weather-charts, on which they carefully set down the date and time when they made their first readings.

"I shan't mind if it rains now," laughed Mandy. "It'll give us something to measure."

"We must go down last thing with a torch to take the temperature before we go to bed," said Ilma, and Mandy nodded.

It was dusk when the girls took the torch and went down the garden to take a final reading for the day. As Ilma climbed the ladder, something stung her eyes, and then she saw smoke coming from the garden next door. Straining her eyes, she saw that it was billowing out of the shed.

"Mandy," she called out to her sister, "Mr Bennett's garden-shed's on fire! We'd better go and——" She broke off, then let out a gasp.

"What is it?" cried Mandy.

"It's Mr Bennett! He's in there! When the fire blazed up for a minute I saw him. He's inside, lying on the floor. Come on, Mandy! We've got to pull him out."

There was a high fence between the two gardens. Hurriedly descending the ladder, Ilma carried it over to the fence, with the help of Mandy. Then she ran up it and, standing for an instant on the top of the fence, jumped down into the next-door garden.

"Shall I go and tell Mum?" Mandy called out.

"No—no time! Come on over!" Ilma called back urgently. "We've got to get Mr Bennett out. He may suffocate if he's

"It's Mr Bennett! He's in there!" cried Ilma

left in all that smoke."

Mandy realised that Ilma was right. The smoke was pouring out of the shed. Fanned by the wind that blew in through the half-open door, the fire had taken fierce hold of the shed.

Ilma started back for an instant when she reached the shed. The heat was intense and the smoke blinding. But through the haze she could see the still form of Mr Bennett lying on the floor, dangerously near the flames that were leaping up the sides of the shed.

"Give me a hand, Mandy!" she cried. "I'll never be able to move him by myself."

Courageously, she ran into the shed. Remembering what she had learned at Guides, she dropped on to hands and knees and crawled towards Mr Bennett, so staying below the smoke. She grabbed Mr Bennett by the feet and began to pull him towards the door. Then she heard Mandy, who was standing wide-eyed and rather white-faced outside.

"Duck down and help me drag him out, Mandy," she gasped, choking as the smoke enveloped her. "I can hardly move him."

Mandy wasn't very big, but she was as brave as her sister, and she followed Ilma's example, dropped to her knees and, keeping her head well down, inched her way forward. Grabbing the leg Ilma released, she pulled with all her strength. The extra bit of weight and power made just the difference, and between them they managed to pull the unconscious man through the door and into the reviving air.

"He's safe now, anyhow," muttered Ilma, gasping and panting. "Jolly well done, Mandy! I couldn't have got him out without you."

"I'll go and ask Mum to phone for the fire-brigade," said Mandy, and raced away.

Ilma, who had borne more of the heat and smoke than Mandy, stayed where she was, face blackened and still half-choked with the smoke that had gone into her lungs.

How long it was she didn't know, but suddenly she heard the fire-brigade bell clanging, and then saw her father and mother running towards her through Mr Bennett's side gate. She was able to grin weakly as they helped her up to her feet. Then the firemen arrived, and turned hoses on to the shed, which was now ablaze from end to end.

Next, an ambulance arrived, and Mr Bennett was taken away on a stretcher.

In something over an hour the fire was out and Ilma and Mandy were telling what had happened.

"You saved Mr Bennett's life," the fire-brigade captain told the girls. "There's no doubt about that."

The smoke had made the old man unconscious, although, thanks to Ilma and Mandy, he hadn't come to any great harm. It seemed likely that he had fallen asleep in the shed and that his pipe had set fire to wood shavings. It would have been a much more tragic story if the fire hadn't been seen in time and Mr Bennett rescued.

"If we hadn't been doing our weather-chart, we shouldn't have seen the fire," Ilma told them.

The firemen were very interested, and told Ilma and Mandy that they could come to the fire-station and look round it, perhaps even ride on the fire-engine.

A few days later the girls were

Ilma and Mandy were fascinated with Mr Bennett's hobby, which was making pottery

surprised by a visit from Mr Bennett, who had soon recovered in hospital. He had come round to thank them for their timely help.

"I'm told I owe my life to you two," he said gruffly, but with a kindly twinkle in his eyes. "Well, I'm very grateful."

The girls found themselves chatting to the old man quite happily. Mr Bennett was very interested in the weather-station.

"That's a good hobby," he said. "Would you both like to come round and see my hobby some time? It'll be in my house until I can get a new garden-shed put up," he explained.

Both Ilma and Mandy were fascinated with Mr Bennett's hobby of pottery-making. He had created some beautiful things.

"This is a good hobby," he told them. "Would you like me to show you how to do it some time?"

"Oh, yes, please," said both girls together.

"We'll start with something simple, like a mug," said Mr Bennett. "Later on you'll be able to make all sorts of things."

"That'll be lovely," said Ilma. "Thank you very much, Mr Bennett."

"It's not much in return for what you did for me," said the old man. "By the way," he added, "if you girls would like to play in my wild garden, you're very welcome at any time."

They accepted eagerly.

Mr Bennett smiled. "I've been rather a hermit lately. Perhaps you two will help to bring me out of my shell."

"I'm a Guide," Ilma told him, "and my sister will be one soon. We'd love to make a shelter in your garden and perhaps have a Patrol den there."

"You can have the run of the wild part of the garden," he told them. "So long as you keep to the wild part you can do what you like."

"We'll make a Patrol den there," Ilma confided to Mandy, "and when you join Guides you can come in with us. I'm sure our Guider will let you join my Patrol."

"I shall like that," said Mandy. "But between now and then I'm going to enjoy my weather-station."

Picture Jigsaw

To fit the jigsaw together, copy the drawing in each square in the blank frame below with the same number; then you will see the complete picture

Slow Coach Puzzle

Take out twelve pairs of words that usually go together—like MATCH and STICK. What are you left with?

House Crossword
by Helen N. Martindale

Clues Across
1—Guides like to camp by these
5—A long word that means able to do things well
6—Signal of distress
7—Don't forget to wipe your feet on this

Clues Down
1—On your feet
2—You use these when you learn knotting
3—Put your photographs in this
4—You follow this with your nose

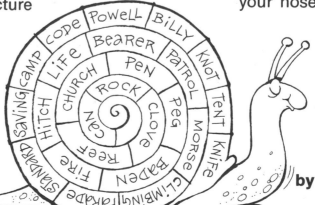

by L. M. Jones

CAN YOU NAME THE

by M. I. Eckhardt

Can you name the trees in the wood from these pictures of them or from their leaves? That's what Jane and Tina are trying to do. Then they're going to learn more about each tree. They're both Wide-Awake Brownies.

If you name each tree correctly and write in the names on the leaf, you will form the name of the eighth tree in the wood.

REES IN THE WOOD?

CLUES

1. It's a tree with "keys" on it
2. It sounds as if it grows by the sea, but it doesn't
3. Ships used to be made from this mighty tree, which bears acorns
4. Another name for this is the linden tree
5. It's prickly, an evergreen, and popular at Christmas
6. It's silvery and graceful
7. It lives to a great age, is often found in churchyards, and provided the wood for old English archers' bows
8. It has "wings" on it

ANSWERS

1—ash, 2—beech, 3—oak, 4—lime, 5—holly, 6—birch, 7—yew, 8—sycamore

Cycling Quiz

by George H. Haines

If you are a cyclist, see if you can get four correct answers to this quiz.

2. Which hazard are you meant to look out for first—children or cows?

3. In which lane should you ride a cycle on a motorway?

4. What is wrong with this old notice?

1. What is the meaning of the signal this policeman is giving?

BRIDLE ROAD ONLY
NO
CARS OR CYCLES

It's Not What It Seems!

Says Daphne M. Pilcher

What Is It?

1. What is a cabbage white when it is not a white cabbage?
2. What was a kipper before it was a kipper?
3. What is a lark when it's not a bit of fun?
4. What is a lady's slipper when it isn't worn by a lady?
5. What is a crane when it isn't a machine for moving heavy weights
6. What is a bluebottle when it isn't a bottle coloured blue?
7. What is old man's beard when it's not an old man's beard?
8. What is a black widow when she's not a lady?
9. When is a red hot poker not a red hot poker?
10. What is a painted lady when it is not a lady's portrait?

Word Puzzle

by R. E. Knight

Can you find five winged creatures from the numbers in the squares? The answer to 1 DOWN is BAT, and the middle creature is a bird with a yellow beak. Now puzzle the others out.

	2 5						4 23	
1 2	12	1	3	3 11	2	9	18	4
1		7		9			5	
20		12		20			14	
		5		5				

The Pool Challenge

by Jean Hopkins

"It's no use." Angela clenched her teeth and tried hard not to cry.

Her best friend, Rebecca, took her arm and helped her from the pool. "Don't worry, Angela," she said. "You'll do it next week."

Angela nodded—she could not trust herself to speak; she was too upset. Class 6 at Springleaze School were having their weekly swimming lesson, and for the third week running Mrs Farrel had tested Angela for her Brownie swimming badge.

Angela could do everything else quite easily, even diving off the springboard, but she could not pick up the brick from the bottom of the pool. She hated the feel of the water going over her mouth and up her nose.

"I'll never be able to do it," thought Angela as she hurried to towel herself dry and get back for school dinner. Brown Owl would be sure to ask if she had done it this time.

However, at Brownies next day her Brownie Guider, Mrs Lake, had some exciting news. During half term the Brownies were to have an outing to the sea for a day. They would travel by coach, take a packed lunch and be back by tea-time. The Brownies were very excited and talked eagerly of what they would like to do. They could play rounders on the beach, collect shells, go in the pool. The Brownie Guider gave them all the details, and the Brownies carefully wrote everything in their notebooks.

Rebecca and Angela could talk of nothing else after the Brownie meeting.

"Wonder if we'll see any crabs," Rebecca said.

"Hope they won't be big ones," replied her friend. "We might get some more pretty pebbles for our collection."

"At the seaside I could buy Colin a bucket for his birthday," said Rebecca.

"Oh, yes," agreed Angela. "There are sure to be buckets there."

Rebecca's little brother badly wanted a bucket for his sandpit. It was his birthday in two weeks' time, and Rebecca had been saving her pocket-money for weeks. She and Angela spent a very happy hour counting all Rebecca's money and sorting out their pebble collection.

At last the happy day arrived, and all the Brownies gathered on the village green to await the coach. Many mothers came to wave them off, and several little sisters looked enviously on and wished they were seven and could be Brownies too. Mrs Lake checked names and sorted out the coach-money. Soon they were off. The journey passed quickly as there was so much to see out of the windows. At last they spied the sea. It came nearer and nearer. At last the coach drove on to the promenade, and the driver opened the door.

"See you at four o'clock," he said.

"Beach first," said Mrs Lake. "You may wander along the beach, but keep in twos and go no farther than the pier. I shall sit here by the pool to watch those who wish to go in." Some rocks had been hollowed out to form a small pool, which was filled by the tide each day.

The Brownies disappeared very quickly. Everyone had something special to do: some to collect shells, some to buy rock, or have donkey-rides. Mrs Lake sat surrounded by coats and lunch-packs. She watched Angela and Rebecca make for the pool. After a while she saw that Rebecca was shivering.

"Come out now, dear," she called. "You look cold."

Rebecca soon dried herself. She took up her purse, as she was eager to buy Colin's bucket.

"I'll come out now," called Angela.

"Here's your towel," called out Rebecca, and she ran to the pool. Suddenly there was a splash, and Rebecca's purse with all her money inside fell into the pool.

Rebecca burst into tears. The money for Colin's bucket was in the purse. What could she do?

"Don't cry, Rebecca," said Angela. "I'll get it for you. Yes, here it is; I can feel it with my feet." Without hesitating, she bent down and picked the purse off the bottom.

"You may wander along the beach," said Mrs Lake. "I shall sit by the pool and watch"

Rebecca smiled through her tears. What a relief it was to get the purse back! What a wonderful friend Angela was!

Mrs Lake came running up to see what was happening. She comforted Rebecca. Angela dried herself and changed back into her uniform. They spread Rebecca's wet money out on a towel and counted it. Rebecca was very relieved to find it was all there. Mrs Lake found an old envelope in her handbag, and Rebecca put the money in it.

"Your purse will soon dry out if you peg it on the line at home," said Mrs Lake as she wrapped it up with the wet swimming things. "Now off you go and buy that bucket before anything else happens."

They hurried off towards the gay beach-stall, which was full of balls, spades, buckets and other things needed for the seaside.

They waved to Mrs Lake as they returned with a large parcel. Two beaming Brownies sat down and showed her the lovely blue bucket Rebecca had bought.

"Colin will love it," said Mrs Lake. "He's lucky to have such a kind sister. And, Angela," she continued, "do you realise that you picked something from the bottom of the pool today, just as you have to for the Swimmer badge?"

Angela looked puzzled for a moment, and then she beamed. "Goodness, so I did!" she exclaimed. "I can do it, after all."

The other Brownies had all gathered round by this time, eager to see Rebecca's new bucket and to show their own treasures from the beach. Then sandwiches were unpacked, and all the Brownies proved that they

They spread Rebecca's wet money out on a towel and counted it

46

were ravenous. They spent further happy hours and ended with a game of rounders. Rebecca clutched her precious bucket tightly as they all boarded the coach for home.

After the half-term holiday, swimming lessons soon came round for Class 6. This time Mrs Farrel was not in any doubt. She had heard about Angela's recovery of the purse from Rebecca.

"You first, Angela," she said, "and we will start with the brick." She threw it in and it sank to the bottom. "Come along, dear!" she called.

Angela stood and looked at the brick. She half closed her eyes and tried to imagine that the brick was a purse—Rebecca's purse, with all her savings in. Down she went, and as easily as winking she grasped the brick and pulled it out.

Her friends cheered. "Hooray, hooray!"

"You can do it, after all!" smiled Mrs Farrel. "You've proved you can do it."

MY BROWNIE SIX
by Allison J. Young
a Ghillie Dhu of the 3rd St. Ninian's Pack, Stirling, Scotland

The Kelpies are a merry Six,
Full of fun and full of tricks.
They jump about from noon till night,
But I would rather be a Sprite.

A Sprite does lots of good, good deeds,
Helping others in their needs.
She helps all other Brownie Sixes,
Though I prefer the tiny pixies.

A Pixie sits in Pow-wow Ring,
Learning music and how to sing.
The Pixie helps both me and you,
But I just love the Ghillie Dhu.

The Ghillie Dhu is a friendly thing;
Lots of pleasure does it bring.
I go to Brownies now with zest;
The Ghillie Dhu do I like best.

Allison lives next to the site of the famous battlefield of Bannockburn

Shopping Basket Picture Crossword

The farmer's wife went shopping in the market-town.

What did she buy? You can find out from the picture clues. Write your answers in the numbered spaces in the basket, down and across.

by Brenda Morton

ACROSS

DOWN

The coatimundi hurries out of the undergrowth to find out what all the noise is about

A HAPPY ZOO YEAR

for the St. Clare's (Preston) Pack

With photographs by Michael Edwards

The horned owl is cross at being disturbed

Nicola Bridge makes friends with Lollipop

For their first outing since the Pack was formed, the 2nd Fulwood (St. Clare's) Brownies, of Preston, Lancashire, visited Chester Zoo. There a surprise awaited them. They were taken into the animals' kitchen, where all kinds of strange and unusual foods are prepared for the zoo inhabitants.

There were apples by the hundred, huge bags of carrots and oranges, masses of yellow bananas, and strings of juicy grapes. All the fruit looked so tempting that the Brownies could have eaten it themselves!

The Brownies were given feed-trays and were then allowed to prepare the food by slicing it into pieces and sharing it out for each group of animals. They must have made a good job

of it because the animals gobbled everything up with relish.

At Chester Zoo creatures from all over the world can be seen with only water between them and the visitors. Channels of water separate them instead of bars, which is much better for everybody.

There was another sur-

The lady keeper introduces the baby chimps, Jamie and Lollipop, to Laura Edwards and Judith O'Brien

prise in store for the Brownies. A keeper brought out two baby chimps, Lollipop and Jamie, and, as you can see in the pictures, the Brownies soon made friends with them. The chimps were shy at first, but there's nothing like a bit of fun to break the ice, and soon they were romping about with the Brownies and thoroughly enjoying themselves. One creature, though, wasn't amused. He was a horned owl, who didn't care two hoots about the Brownies' visit. "You've got your own Brown Owl," he muttered

"Shall we dance?"

to himself, "so don't bother me." He shut his eyes and went off to sleep.

The Brownies were sorry to say goodbye to the friendly chimps, and the

After play, a hug

monkeys next door chattered loudly at them as they left, as much as to say, "Do come again soon, and bring some more of that luscious fruit with you!"

Wherever Lucy went she was always the smallest. She was the smallest in the family. She was the smallest in her class at school. She was the smallest in her Brownie Pack, although she was ten and a Second.

She hated being teased about her small size. Even more, she hated it when people, who meant to be kind, said, "Never mind, Lucy, the most precious things are wrapped up in small parcels."

Each year, early in December, the District Guides and Scouts put on a show at the local theatre. Usually it was a Christmas play. Sometimes there were Brownie Guides and Cub Scouts in the chorus.

In November, the Brownie Guider told the Pack: "The Guides and Scouts are putting on a musical play early in December. Mr Rogers is the producer. He needs some Brownies who can sing and dance, but they must be old enough to go to the evening rehearsals. Let me know if any of you would like to go to be tried for a part."

Nicola said that she would like to be in the play. She was a tall, thin girl and a keen dancer. She said, "I think my mother would let me go to the rehearsals if I had a friend to go with me."

"I'll come with you," Lucy offered.

Nicola's mother took the two Brownies to the theatre. The auditorium looked very big and dusty with its rows of empty seats. There was a piano on the stage, and a small group of girls were dancing. In the front row, by the empty music-stands, Mr Rogers was talking to some Cub Scouts who had been chosen to be golliwogs and teddy bears for

JUST THE RIGHT SIZE

BY NORA WINDRIDGE

a toyshop scene. The Brownie Guider was there, and she hurried Nicola on to the stage.

"Come along, Nicola; they are going to choose six singing rabbits."

Lucy stood back and watched with interest.

Mr Rogers said to the Cub Scouts: "Run along now. Be here on Friday at half-past six for rehearsal." He turned round and saw Lucy. He said, "Hello! What do you do?"

"Me?" asked Lucy.

"You look just right for the small girl in a nightie; she gets lost in a wood, holding her teddy bear. It's quite an important part." He smiled at Lucy. "All the Guides are too big for the part. How old are you?"

"I'm ten," Lucy replied. When she said, "I'm ten," most people

said, "Are you, really?" in a surprised way.

But Mr Rogers said, "Are you, really?" in a very pleased voice. He explained: "I need a girl who *looks* quite small and young but who is really old enough to come to evening rehearsals. Can you act?"

"I don't know," answered Lucy honestly She hadn't expected a part in the play.

"Take this book. It's a copy of the play. Turn to page four and read it to me."

Lucy took the book and read to him.

"H'm! Not bad. You'll need lots of practice and you'll have to speak out loudly, but I think you'll do. You're just right to play Annabel—just the right size."

Just the right size! That's what

"Hello! What do you do?" asked Mr Rogers

Lucy had always wanted to be!

Nicola came down the steps, eyes and feet still dancing.

"I'm to be in the chorus, Lucy—a singing rabbit! I have to dance too! The play is about three children. The littlest one is Annabel."

"I'm . . . I'm Annabel," said Lucy.

"Annabel gets lost in a wood," continued Nicola, "and . . . and . . . what did you say, Lucy?"

"I'm Annabel."

"Really and truly?"

"I'm just the right size," Lucy explained. "Mr Rogers said so. Just the right size, he said."

"Golly!" said Nicola. "How super! Just the right size!"

51

These Brownies from the 31st and 64th Portsmouth Packs try on helmets on a visit to the Winchester fire-station, but find it hard to get a good fit

Colour print by Miss W. J. Beer

At their Thinking Da party the 1st Norha Brownies, Northumbe land, dress up in th national costumes of va ous countries and mak very picturesque grou

Colour print by Mrs L.

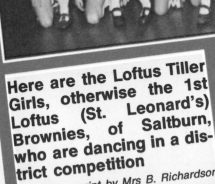

Here are the Loftus Tiller Girls, otherwise the 1st Loftus (St. Leonard's) Brownies, of Saltburn, who are dancing in a district competition

Colour print by Mrs B. Richardson

Another Pack, the 142nd Sheffield (Frecheville), become Brownies of other lands on Thinking Day, complete with Sunbeam and other badges

Colour print by Mrs S. R. Millward

Dressing Up! and All Our Own Work!

Interesting and artistic displays of work by the 12th Loughborough Y.W.C.A Brownies

Colour print by Miss A. Hallam

Four Brownies of the 5th Stockton (St. Peter's) Pack clean the church brass as a Lent Venture, closely watched by the Pack Leader

Colour print by Miss J. Lambert

53

FUN WITH LEAVES

L. BAKER Shows You How to Arrange Autumn Leaves and Fruits for the Collector Badge

You can make an interesting collection of autumn leaves and fruits in the following way.

Ask Daddy or Mummy to give you a polystyrene tile, large or small, depending on how big your collection is intended to be. Collect autumn leaves of different colours and shapes, or an assortment of seeds and fruits that fall off the trees in autumn.

The tile can be left white, but it looks very pretty if painted first with poster-paint. Choose a colour to contrast with the leaves and fruits. Leave the tile to dry after painting it.

Choose the best positions for your leaves and fix them securely with drawing-pins. These go easily into the tile. If you have two leaves of the same shape, one slightly larger than the other, place the smaller one on top of the larger, pushing in a drawing-pin to secure them in position. This gives a kind of three-dimensional effect.

The leaves can be stuck in position with glue if preferred. A short piece of tape can be fixed to the back of the tile with two drawing-pins, so that your collection can be hung on a wall and be seen and admired.

Don't forget to put the names of the leaves and fruits under them so that everyone will know what they are.

LEAF WRITING

by Elsie Longwood

Dear Ann Please come to tea with me From Jane

"It's not as good as a camp-fire, Mummy"

Here's a new kind of "secret" writing that you will find great fun.

First find a thin stick and gather some big leaves—laurel leaves are much the best—and with your stick write letters upon the backs of the leaves.

At first the writing will not be seen, but if a leaf is left in the sun for a little while the writing turns brown. The longer it is left the darker it becomes, until it looks almost as though ink had been used.

Several letters can be written and placed in a sunny spot in the garden. Soon they will be ready to post. You could arrange a secret postbox with your special friend and send each other "leaf letters".

You will find that it is more fun to write with a stick upon laurel leaves than it is to use ordinary paper and pencil.

Along the Highway

Puzzle by Daphne M. Pilcher

Here are ten places you might see in your journey along a highway. To find out what they are, put a vowel in each circle (that is, A, E, I, O or U) and a consonant (that is, any of the other letters of the alphabet) in the squares.

☐ ◯ ☐ **P** ◯ ☐ ◯ ☐

☐ ☐ ◯ **T** ◯ ◯ ☐

☐ ◯ **N** ◯ ☐ ◯

☐ **H** ◯ ☐

☐ ◯ ☐ **K**

☐ **H** ◯ ☐ ☐ ☐

☐ ◯ ☐ ◯ **G** ◯

☐ ◯ **B** ☐ ◯ ☐ ☐

☐ ◯ **W** ☐ ☐ ◯ ☐ ☐

F ◯ ☐ ☐ ◯ ☐ ☐

Name the Animals
by Ruth Hoult

To find the animals, match up the squares in the left column with those on the right.

ST	REW
OT	DGER
SH	TER
BA	BBIT
WE	OAT
RA	ASEL

Which Two Are Alike?
by Irene Urquhart

Look closely at the nine designs and see if you can find which two are alike.

NATURE TRAIL TO THE BROWNIE MOTTO

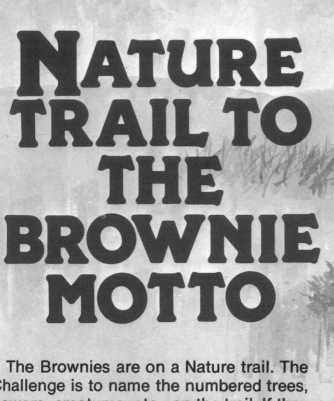

START

The Brownies are on a Nature trail. The Challenge is to name the numbered trees, flowers, creatures, etc., on the trail. If they are correctly named, the first letter of each put together will make the Brownie motto.

Can *you* follow the trail to the motto? There are two numbers to each item on the trail, so if you can't name one you may know the other.

4

4

5

5

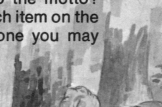

6

6

6

These brief descriptions will help you: 1—reptile with long scaly body and tail; 1—pretty songbird. 2—tree in which rooks love to nest; 2—wriggly fish. 3—pond creature that lives on land and in water; 3—woodland bird with nest in hole of tree. 4—common flowers found in meadows, gardens, etc.; 4—shy animal mostly found in forests. 5—pretty woodland flowers with name hard to say; 5—tree that you might think smoked. 6—large bird that fishes for its meals; 6—fast-running animal with big ears. 7—Britain's only venomous snake; 7—home of colony of busy insects. 8—plants that sting; 8—fruit of the hazel-tree. 9—yellow flowers of meadow, hedgerow and garden; 9—water-birds that say "quack".

The Good Turn
By H. Wheelhouse

"**I** never seem to be able to find anything to do as a good turn," Carrie confided to Stella, as they put on their coats after the Saturday-morning Pack meeting.

"*I* never find any trouble in doing good turns," returned Stella. "I hardly ever miss doing a good turn every day."

Carrie looked admiringly at Stella, who had several badges on her arm and was expected to be the new Sixer of the Sprites when Judy went up to Guides. Carrie herself was rather meek, whereas Stella was self-assured —in fact, according to some of the Brownies, stuck-up.

"What kind of good turns do you do?" asked Carrie, as she and Stella walked home together. "If you told me I might be able to think of some to do."

"It's not something you have to think about," replied Stella, in a condescending voice. "Good turns just come to you to do."

Carrie wished she was more like Stella instead of being rather a mouse-like Brownie. She brightened up when Stella said: "I'm going to do another good turn after lunch. I'm calling for Mrs Turner's groceries and taking them up to her. She lives by herself on Mossleigh Hill. You could come with me."

"Be very careful when you cross the stream," Mr Lane warned Stella

"Oh, could I? Thank you, Stella."

The two Brownies met after lunch at Mr Lane's grocery store. Mr Lane had a large basket of groceries waiting for them. "Be very careful, especially when you cross the stream," he warned Stella. "We don't want Mrs Turner's weekly supplies sailing down the stream, do we?"

The walk up the hill was very enjoyable to Carrie. Stella let her hold one part of the handle of the basket, and she felt that she was sharing the good turn until, near the top of the hill, Stella took over the basket.

"It's my good turn," she said. "I must hand over the basket to Mrs Turner myself."

"Yes, of course, Stella," said Carrie meekly, but she felt a little stab of disappointment at not being able to share the good turn right to the end.

Mrs Turner saw them coming and greeted them with a wave. "You are a good girl, Stella," she said. "And you've brought a friend with you this time. Come in and have a drink and a biscuit or two."

"Stella has let me help her do her good turn today," Carrie explained to Mrs Turner, as they ate and drank. "I don't seem able to find good turns to do."

"I expect you will if you are willing to do them," said Mrs Turner, looking at her with shrewd old eyes. "There are lots of good turns that need doing."

"Oh, yes, I'm always finding good turns to do," put in Stella.

Soon after this, they picked up the basket and set off back down the hill. When they came to the wooden bridge over the stream, they stopped and looked over to see if they could see any fish.

"There's one!" cried Stella, leaning over and pointing.

She did not hear the old wooden rails creak. Then suddenly there was a loud crack. The top rail broke sharply. Stella screamed. She tried to keep her balance, but failed. Before Carrie's horrified eyes, she toppled into the stream. She landed full-length on the bed of the stream, which was shallow but stony.

Carrie scrambled down the bank and stretched out her arms to help Stella up and out.

Dripping wet, and grazed by the stones, Stella stood on the bank and cried.

"Never mind," Carrie comforted her. "We'll soon get home if we run. I'll carry the basket, Stella, and I'll take it back to Mr Lane for you."

Still sobbing, Stella let Carrie take her hand and lead her away. Her mother took her in and comforted her. "Thank you for helping her, Carrie," she said, after the Brownie explained what had happened.

Carrie took the basket back to the grocery store and handed it to Mr Lane, who asked where Stella was and whether the groceries had been safely delivered. Carrie had to explain about the mishap.

"I see," said Mr Lane. "So you were the one to do the good turn today!"

"So I was," thought Carrie happily, as she made her way home. "Stella's good turn was taking the basket to Mrs Turner, but I did a good turn by pulling Stella out of the stream."

Carrie scrambled down the bank to help Stella up and out

OURS IS A NICE

In the Surrey village of Normandy stands a Brownie-size house specially made to fit children. It is built of pine in period style, is two stories high, and is fully furnished even to the kitchen stove. Close to it is a

It's what house-agents would call a desirable period house with all mod cons

Inside it's nicely furnished with rustic tables and chairs and wall-to-wall carpets

Colour slides by Alan T. Band Associates

'OUSE, OURS IS

child-size house built in a tree—or, rather, between two trees linked by a wooden bridge, along which you walk to enter it. The houses were built by Mr Leslie Bayliss for his children, who play and eat in them.

The old-fashioned kitchen stove is in keeping with the period of the house

There is no shortage of visitors to the exciting tree-house

T.J. JENNINGS TELLS YOU

HOW ANIMALS TALK TO EACH OTHER

When animals talk to each other they do not always use their voices. This is not quite so strange as it may at first seem when you think how easy it is to "talk" with someone else through gestures, changes in your face and head movements.

Most of the sounds animals make are rather like the first efforts of a baby to speak. They are sounds rather than words. One reason why animals do not use words as we know them is because their lips are not suited to shaping words.

The sounds animals make seem more or less the same all the time to our ears, but animals' senses are generally much more acute than ours. Animals can distinguish changes of tone which we can't.

It is easy to understand the language of dogs and cats. We know that when a cat purrs it is pleased and that when it hisses and arches its back it is angry. Cats and dogs have been pets of man for thousands of years, so it is not so surprising that we should have learned to understand some of their language.

The speech of most wild animals and birds is not nearly so easy to understand. When you hear the rich, sweet whistle of the blackbird you may think it is a song of happiness, but it is more likely to be a warning to other birds to keep out of its chosen territory. The loud, clattering alarm cry of a startled blackbird sends other birds and animals scuttling for cover. Many poachers, foxes and cats must have gone hungry as a result of a blackbird's warning cry.

All the birds and the higher animals use their voices. The giraffe is voiceless, but the mother can communicate with her young. Even whales make noises to each other. When a special microphone was lowered into the sea near a "school" of whales a variety of whistling and warbling noises were heard.

Grasshoppers, crickets and locusts make noises by rubbing their hind legs against their wings. They also have "ears" on or near their knees.

Small insects such as ants make no sounds which we can hear. Doubtless they are able to talk to each other, since when two ants meet they stop and gently touch each other with their antennae. This may be a special method of conversing.

Bees have a most remarkable method of "speaking". If a bee returns to the hive with a plentiful supply of nectar and pollen, it tells the others where to find it by dancing. From this special kind of dance the other bees are able to tell in which direction and how far away the nectar and pollen are.

The bat "talks to itself", although this is not language in the ordinary sense. As it moves through the air, the bat makes high-pitched squeaking noises. These sounds are reflected back from obstacles and caught in its sensitive ears. From the length of time it takes for the echoes to come back the bat knows how far it is from the obstacles and is thus able to avoid them. This method is copied in the echo-sounding apparatus now used in ships.

If you wish to talk to animals it doesn't matter so much what words you use, but rather the way in which you use them. Your own pet dog or cat knows immediately whether you are pleased or cross without your having to say a word. Other animals and birds know your feelings from the way you speak to them.

Photographs
by
Alan T. Band
Associates

When You Go Up to Guides

All kinds of new and exciting activities await you in Guides—hiking, orienteering, camping, as well as interesting indoor work and play. A few of them are pictured on this and the opposite page.

Like these Guides, you may try your hand at cooking in a biscuit-tin oven

Colour print by Mrs P. Pescod

You'll join in planning Patrol activities, which is what these Reigate Guides are doing

Colour print by Miss B. Wing

You'll learn about colours, which the Patrol Leader in this picture is explaining to her Patrol how to fold and fly

Colour print by Miss B. Wing

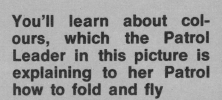

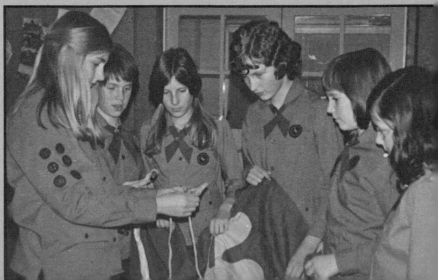

The Patrol Leader lists items to be packed for camp

Photograph by Kent Messenger

At camp you'll share the pleasant chore of adding to the woodpile

In Guides you may even join a Guide/Scout band and compete in the National Band Champlonships

Photograph by courtesy of Surrey Advertiser

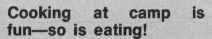

Cooking at camp is fun—so is eating!

Photograph by Mrs J. Tupper

LITTLE DOG LOST

A Brownie Adventure in Pictures by ROBERT MOSS
Based on a Story by Christine Hornsby

OH, NO! DO SAY IT'S NOT YOU, SPRITE! YOU'RE NOT COCOA, ARE YOU?

LOST
BROWN ROUGH-HAIRED PUPPY.
CHILD'S PET ANSWERS TO NAME OF COCOA
MAXTON, LANCETON HOUSE, PICTON.

SPRITE ANSWERS THE DESCRIPTION OF THE LOST PUPPY, DEBBIE, SO WE MUST TAKE HIM TO LANCETON HOUSE TO MAKE SURE.

I—I SUPPOSE SO, MUMMY, BUT I DO HOPE HE ISN'T THE ONE.

WHY, IT'S COCOA! OH, YOU'VE BROUGHT HIM BACK!

THIS IS A WONDERFUL DAY FOR JANET. SHE'S PINED FOR COCOA.

WHEN I THOUGHT SPRITE — THAT IS, COCOA — WAS RACING AFTER A RABBIT HE MUST HAVE RECOGNISED WHERE HE WAS AND WAS REALLY RUNNING HOME.

I'VE MISSED HIM SO MUCH, BUT I'D LOVE YOU TO SHARE HIM WITH ME, DEBBIE, AS HE'S AS MUCH YOURS AS MINE NOW.

WAVE GOODBYE, COCOA!

JANET WANTS TO JOIN BROWNIES, MUM, AND BE IN MY SIX, THE SPRITES.

IT SEEMS TO ME YOU'VE LOST A DOG AND FOUND A FRIEND, DEBBIE.

FUNFARE

RIDDLES

At what time of day was Adam created?
A little before Eve.

What kind of ears does an engine have?
Engineers.

What makes dentists seem so sad?
Because they look down in the mouth.

If a butcher is six feet tall and wears an apron, what does he weigh?
Meat.

— DODSWORTH —

"We'll have to re-pitch our tent!"

The Secret

A Play by Angela De Soyza

A Brownie of the 12th Glenrothes Pack, Fife

Scene One: *In the sitting-room*
MOTHER: Jane, Peter, would you like to go and pick brambles?
JANE: Yes, of course we would.
PETER: Can we have bramble pie for tea?
MOTHER: Yes. You may get your baskets and you can go to the woods at the back of the house.
The children get their baskets
JANE: Goodbye, Mummy.
MOTHER: Remember to be back before it is dark.

Scene Two: *In the woods*
JANE: There are no brambles here.
PETER: Let's go further into the woods.
JANE: Yes, that's a good idea.
The children walk further into the woods
JANE: There are plenty of brambles here.
PETER: Yes, and they are very big.
The children pick for a few minutes
JANE: Ouch! My finger!
PETER: I've half-filled my basket. Let's fill them and then go home.

JANE: When the baskets are full we'll go home.
PETER: Yes; come on, then.
The children walk for a few minutes
JANE: Peter, we turned left here.
PETER: No, it was not. We turned right.
Peter and Jane walk along
JANE: I don't remember these trees.
PETER: Neither do I, but come on.
A little later. Backstage a witch's laugh
PETER: Jane, did you hear that noise?
JANE: No. It must be your imagination.
Same noise again
PETER: Did you hear it?
JANE: Yes, I did.
PETER: It came from over there. Let's go and see.
JANE (trembling): All right, then.
They go to where the noise came from
Scene Three: *Behind some big rocks*
JANE: Can you see what I see?
PETER: Yes. Be quiet.

They see a witch sitting at her cauldron
WITCH: Lizards' cottons
Make a fine pair of stockens.
I see you, my hearties
—come!

Scene Four: *In the witch's cave*
WITCH: Sit down.
Jane and Peter obey
WITCH: Well, how did you come to be here?
JANE: Well, you see, we were picking brambles and we lost our way.
WITCH: Where do you live?
PETER: We live by the park.
WITCH: Here is a map. Follow the directions and you will be home.
PETER: Thank you.
JANE: I thought witches were bad.
WITCH: Not all witches. Now away home! Come and see me again.
Jane and Peter followed the directions and got home safely. They did not tell anyone about the witch. When they were on holiday they went to see the witch, and even had tea with her.

THINKING DAY

Lisa Burkinshaw, of the 142nd Sheffield (Frecheville) Pack, lights her Thinking Day candle for "Mother Sun" and all the Sunbeams in Africa and recites two of the Sunbeam rhymes:

We're the Raindrops small and neat;
When we fall we cool your feet.

We're the Rainbows smiling bright,
Though the clouds be dark as night.

Brownies escort the Mayor and Mayoress from the church after the Hove Division's Thinking Day service

HETTY'S HALLOWE'EN

by Nora Windridge

"Wait till Hallowe'en," her friends in second grade told Hetty.

"What happens at Hallowe'en?" Hetty asked.

"Wait and see!"

Hetty was an English Brownie who had come to Canada for a year with her mother and father and her little brother, Joe. She started school and joined the local Brownie Pack.

Soon it was October—or, as Canadians call it, the fall—when the wind blows cold but the skies are bright-blue and the leaves are brown, orange and gloriously red.

"What happens at Hallowe'en?" Hetty asked her mother.

"Wait and see! Already the supermarket is hung with models of black cats and witches, and is stocked with great bags of candy kisses, hard and sticky."

Hetty's friends told her: "You will need fancy dress and a mask for Hallowe'en, and ask your mother to buy some apples and put some pennies by."

"I thought she was a witch," Joe whispered to Hetty

"Whatever does happen at Hallowe'en?" thought Hetty curiously.

On Hallowe'en, October 31st, Hetty and her Brownie friends hurried home from school.

"We'll call for you at six," they told her. "Be ready and bring a bag."

Mummy and Joe had polished apples and pennies till they shone. They put them in a basket by the front door with chewing-gum and candy kisses. Mummy had made a big Red Riding Hood cloak for Hetty.

"You must wear your warm trousers too," she said, "and your boots and mitts."

"I'm coming too!" cried Joe. He was dressed as a pirate, with a red kerchief on his head and a wooden cutlass stuck into the bright sash tied round his anorak.

When Hetty's father came home he carried a Jack-o'-lantern and set it in the window of the darkened sitting-room. It was a pumpkin hollowed out and with a lighted candle inside.

"That's to show that we're keeping Hallowe'en tonight," he said.

Joe and Hetty waited by the curtains in the yellow pumpkin glow.

"Here they come!" Hetty cried.

Outside in the darkness they saw three Brownies. Karen and Nancy wore masks with painted faces and were dressed in fancy costumes. Pam was a Japanese lady. Nancy looked like a fairy, but all wore their warm furry hoods and mitts as well. Karen wore a tall hat and dark cloak.

Joe shivered when he saw her. "I thought she was a witch," he whispered to Hetty.

"Wait!" Mother said. "Don't

At every house they were given "treats": apples or pennies or candies

open the front door yet."

So they waited till the doorbell rang. As Mother opened it the Brownies shouted out: "Trick or treat!"

"How will you pay me?"

"With a song," they said, and sang a verse of *Jack-o'-lantern shining in your yellow field.*

Hetty giggled in the shadows. Mother gave the girls their "treats": a polished apple and a shiny penny.

"Now," she said to Hetty, "take your carrier-bag and hold Joe's hand."

So they all ran off: five of them now—Karen, Nancy and Pam, and Hetty and Joe.

At every house where Jack-o'-lanterns shone they climbed the steps, rang the bell, and shouted out: "Trick or treat!"

Sometimes they sang or recited verses or asked a riddle. Karen knew a lot of riddles. At every house they were given "treats": apples or pennies or candies. Other girls and boys joined them, Sally, Peter, Mark, Jenny and Jill. There were eleven of them now in the darkness, painted and masked and dressed up.

"So this is Hallowe'en!" said Hetty. She kept tight hold of Joe.

At last they turned a corner, and Hetty saw to her surprise that they were back in her own street.

"There you are, Hetty and Joe! We've brought you home."

Hetty ran in to show her mother and father the bag of "treats".

"We've decided to put our pennies towards Brownie funds, but we can eat the candies now!"

"Bedtime!" her mother said presently. "Look! Joe is asleep already."

So he was, sitting on the bottom stair, his eyes tightly shut and his face all smeared with paint and candy.

"I like Canadian Hallowe'en," said Hetty happily.

ANSWERS TO PUZZLES

Birds, Moths, Butterflies (pages 8, 9)
Birds: 1—pheasant, 2—pied wagtail, 3—swallow, 4—bluetit, 5—rook, 6—cuckoo, 7—nightingale. *Moths:* 8—emperor moth, 9—lime-hawk moth, 10—tiger moth. *Butterflies:* 11—clouded yellow, 12—tortoiseshell, 13—red admiral

Silhouette Puzzle (page 27)
1—Signaller, 2—Writer, 3—Artist, 4—Athlete, 5—Cyclist, 6—Agility, 7—Skater, 8—Musician, 9—Pathfinder

Find Her Name! (page 27)
Marguerite

House Crossword (page 39)
Across: 1—Streams, 5—Capable, 6—SOS, 7—Mat. *Down:* 1—Socks, 2—Ropes, 3—Album, 4—Scent

Slow Coach Puzzle (page 39)
Life saving, clove hitch, reef knot, church parade, tent peg, Baden Powell, camp fire, Morse code, standard bearer, pen knife, rock climbing, billy can. *Answer:* PATROL

Cycling Quiz (page 42)
1. He is signalling STOP to vehicles in front and behind.
2. Children, then cows. Signs are always in sequence from top to bottom.
3. In none. Cycles are not allowed on motorways.
4. Since the passing of the Countryside Act, 1968, cycles can use bridle roads.

It's Not What It Seems! (page 43)
1—butterfly, 2—herring, 3—bird, 4—wild flower, 5—wading bird, 6—insect, 7—trailing hedgerow plant, 8—spider, 9—garden flower, 10—butterfly

Word Puzzle (page 43)
1—bat, 2—eagle, 3—kite, 4—wren. *Middle Bird:* blackbird

Isle of Man Brownies (1st Jurby) wear the Easter bonnets they paraded to raise funds for a new headquarters in Douglas
Photo: Mrs. Cooke

Shopping Basket Crossword (page 47)

Along the Highway (page 55)
1—Hospital, 2—Station, 3—Cinema, 4—Shop, 5—Park, 6—Church, 7—Garage, 8—Library, 9—Town Hall, 10—Factory

Which Two Are Alike? (page 55)
No's 2 and 7

Name the Animals (page 55)
Stoat, otter, shrew, badger, weasel, rabbit

Nature Trail (pages 56/57)
1—lizard, linnet; 2—elm, eel; 3—newt, nuthatch; 4—daisies, deer; 5—anemone, ash; 6—heron, hare; 7—adder, anthill; 8—nettles, nuts; 9—dandelions, ducks. Motto: Lend a Hand

Pick the Pictures

Win a Bike and £50 in This Exciting New Competition

All you have to do is to put the six delightful pictures on the next two pages in the order in which you like them. For example, if you like **F** best you put **F** as number 1, the letter of your next choice as number 2, and so on down to number 6. Whatever your age you have as much chance as anyone else of winning the wonderful prize of a new bike for yourself and £50 for your Pack.

The Editor has made his choice. If your first choice agrees with his, you will gain three points; if your second agrees with his, you will gain two points; for each of the others that agrees, one point will be awarded. The competitor with the most points will win the grand double prize. Something of equal value to the bike can be chosen, if preferred.

On the page overleaf is space for you to say in not more than fifty words what you like best about the *Brownie Annual*. Take care with this write-up, because it will be taken into account if there are competitors with the same number of points.

Complete both sides of the entry form and post it to "PICK THE PICTURES" PRIZE COMPETITION, PURNELL BOOKS, BERKSHIRE HOUSE, QUEEN STREET, MAIDENHEAD, SL6 1NF, to arrive not later than March 31, 1979. The winner will be notified as soon as possible after this date.

Just put the picture's letter in the order of your choice

1 ....
2 ....
3 ....
4 ....
5 ....
6 ....

THE BROWNIE ANNUAL "PICK THE PICTURES" COMPETITION ENTRY FORM

My name is ....

My address is ....

....

....

....**My age is**............

My Pack is ....

....

My Guider's name and address is ....

....

....

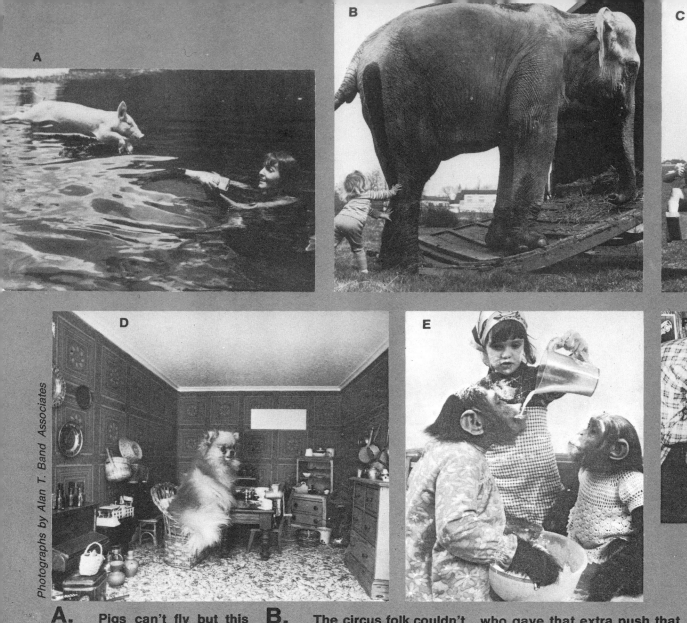

A. Pigs can't fly but this one can jump—even into water if there's milk waiting

B. The circus folk couldn't get the elephant into the van, so they called his friend, Kitty, who gave that extra push that persuaded four tons of elephant to move

What I like best about the *Brownie Annual*

Winner of the 1978 competition was Susan Claire Arescog, of the 26th Kingswood (Wesley) Pack, Bristol.

C. What on earth is this? It's a human roundabout, Walter Cornelius, of Peterborough, who thinks nothing of swinging a couple of children round in swing-boats by man-power only

D. This Pomeranian dog lives a life of luxury in his own house, which is furnished in Victorian style and is, of course, centrally heated

E. Tracey Clews, of Southsea, enjoys cooking, and her pet chimpanzees love helping her to make pastry, especially when a stop is made for drinks

F. Would you believe that there's a college for frogs? Well, here are the pupils, being taught by Professor Steed, of California, U.S.A., to hop in tune with a record

BIBLE CHALLENGE

by Rev. Philip J. Randall

Jesus' ride into Jerusalem on an ass is commemorated at a Palm Sunday service by children carrying palm fronds

Photograph by Alan Band Associates

Here's a new kind of Challenge for your Six or your Pack to try.

The idea is for each Brownie in the Six or the Pack to bring an object mentioned in the Bible and to say where in the Bible the object is mentioned.

For example, you will find that *cups* are mentioned many times in the Bible; so you could take a cup to Pack meeting, together with a note of where in the Bible it is to be found.

Another way would be to think of one of the well-known Bible stories and then take something linked with it—such as a Noah's Ark, with a note that the Ark is written about in Genesis: Chapters 5 to 9.

Here are some more ideas:—

Object	Bible Story	Bible Chapter and Verse
Palm	Jesus' ride into Jerusalem	John: Chapter 12, verses 12-15
2p piece	The Good Samaritan	Luke: Chapter 10, verse 35
5 bread rolls	Feeding of the five thousand	John: Chapter 6, verse 9
Baby doll in basket	Moses in the bulrushes	Exodus: Chapter 2, verse 3
3 smooth stones	David and Goliath	1 Samuel: Chapter 17, verse 40
Bunch of wildflowers	The lilies of the field	Matthew: Chapter 6, verse 28
Seeds	The sower	Mark: Chapter 4, verse 3

Now think about the Bible stories you know and find an object to fit in with one of them.

Photographs: Front endpaper of 1st Birdholme Brownies, Chesterfield, by Miss P. Rothwell, page 3 by *Peterborough Advertiser,* page 78 by *Doncaster Evening Post,* back endpaper by John Warburton